I'm Thankful Each Day!

¡Doy gracias cada día!

I'm Thankful Each Day!

¡Doy gracias cada día!

P. K. Hallinan

ideals children's books.
Nashville, Tennessee

This book is for
Este libro es para

_____

From
De

_____

ISBN-13: 978-0-8249-5583-0

Published by Ideals Children's Books
An imprint of Ideals Publications
A Guideposts Company
Nashville, Tennessee
www.idealsbooks.com

Color separations by Precision Color Graphics, Franklin, Wisconsin
Printed and bound in the U.S.A.

Library of Congress CIP data on file

Worz_Jan12_2

To Parents and Teachers:

I'm Thankful Each Day!, *¡Doy gracias cada día!*, is one of a series of bilingual books specially created by Ideals Children's Books to help children and their parents learn to read both Spanish and English.

Whether the child's native language is English or Spanish, he or she will be able to compare the text and, thus, learn to read both English and Spanish.

Also included at the end of the story are several common words listed in both English and Spanish that the child may review. These include nouns and adjectives, with their gender and number in Spanish, and verbs. In the case of the verbs, the Spanish verbs have the endings that indicate their use in the story.

Parents and teachers will want to use this book as a beginning reader for children who speak either English or Spanish.

A los padres y los maestros:

I'm Thankful Each Day! – *¡Doy gracias cada día!* forma parte de una serie de libros bilingües creados especialmente por Ideals Children's Books para ayudar a los niños y a sus padres a aprender a leer tanto en español como en inglés.

Cualquiera sea su idioma materno, inglés o español, el niño podrá comparar el texto y, de este modo, aprender a leer en ambos idiomas.

Al final de la historia también se incluye una lista de palabras comunes en inglés y español que el niño podrá repasar. Dicha lista contiene sustantivos y adjetivos (con su respectivo género y numero en español) y verbos. Los verbos en español aparecen conjugados tal como se los utiliza en la historia.

Los padres y los maestros podrán usar esta obra como libro de lectura inicial para niños que hablen inglés o español.

I'm thankful each day for the blessings I see,
And for all of the gifts that God's given to me.

Doy gracias cada día por las bendiciones que veo aquí
y por todos los dones que Dios me ha dado a mí.

And counting the stars at the edge of the sea,
I can't help but feel they were put there for me.

Y al contar las estrellas a la orilla del mar,
no puedo evitar sentir que para mí allí están.

I'm thankful for summers
And warm golden days.

Doy gracias por los veranos
y los tibios días dorados.

I'm thankful for autumns
Of orange pumpkin haze.

Doy gracias por la bruma de otoño
de tonos calabaza anaranjados.

I'm thankful for meadows
And bright-colored flowers.

Doy gracias por las praderas
y las flores de colores brillantes.

I'm thankful for raindrops
And soft summer showers.

Doy gracias por las gotas de lluvia
y los aguaceros de verano suaves.

Each sunset is special . . .

Cada atardecer es especial . . .

Each sunrise is new.

Cada amanecer es distinto.

Each breeze in the trees

Is a promise come true.

Cada brisa entre los árboles es

una promesa que realidad se hizo.

Each evening's a wonder
Where beauty abounds.

Cada tarde es un milagro
en donde abunda lo bello.

Each morning's a harvest
Of new sights and sounds.

Cada mañana es una cosecha
de paisajes y sonidos nuevos.

And it's nice just to know that beneath winter's snow
The blossoms of springtime are beginning to grow.

Y es lindo tan solo saber que bajo la nieve de invierno
los capullos de primavera ya están creciendo.

I'm thankful for friends,
For laughing and sharing . . .

Doy gracias por los amigos,
por reír y compartir . . .

I'm thankful for family,

For loving and caring.

Doy gracias por la familia,

por su amor y cariño sentir.

I'm thankful for all
The kindness I see.

Doy gracias pues veo
tanta bondad y ternura.

I'm thankful for peace

And for pure harmony.

Doy gracias por la paz

y la armonía pura.

My body's a present
Of perfect design . . .

Mi cuerpo es un regalo
de diseño perfecto . . .

My mind is a power

As endless as time.

Mi mente es una fuerza

infinita como el tiempo.

And if ever I worry that trouble is near,

I always remember I've nothing to fear . . .

Y si alguna vez me preocupa que el peligro cerca esté,

yo siempre recuerdo que nada tengo que temer . . .

For each hour is laden

With God's perfect love.

Pues cada hora está llena

del amor perfecto de Dios.

Each second brings comfort
And joy from above.

Cada segundo trae del cielo
alegría y consolación.

And I guess in the end the best thing to say

Is I'm thankful for living . . .

Y pienso que, al fin, lo mejor es que diga:

doy gracias por vivir . . .

I'm thankful each day!

¡Doy gracias cada día!

Vocabulary words used in
I'm Thankful Each Day!
¡Doy gracias cada día!

English	Spanish	English	Spanish
I'm thankful	doy gracias	orange	anaranjados
each	cada	pumpkin	calabaza
day	día	haze	bruma
blessings	bendiciones	meadows	praderas
see	veo	bright-colored	de colores brillantes
gifts	dones	flowers	flores
God	Dios	raindrops	gotas de lluvia
counting	contar	soft	suaves
stars	estrellas	showers	aguaceros
edge	orilla	sunset	atardecer
sea	mar	special	especial
help	evitar	sunrise	amanecer
feel	sentir	new	distinto
summers	veranos	breeze	brisa
warm	tibios	trees	árboles
golden	dorados	promise	promesa
autumn	otoño	evening	tarde

English	Spanish	English	Spanish
wonder	milagro	peace	paz
beauty	lo bello	harmony	armonía
abound	abunda	present	regalo
morning	mañana	perfect	perfecto
sights	paisajes	design	diseño
sounds	sonidos	mind	mente
nice	lindo	power	fuerza
know	saber	endless	infinita
beneath	bajo	time	tiempo
winter	invierno	worry	preocupa
snow	nieve	trouble	peligro
blossoms	capullos	remember	recuerdo
springtime	primavera	nothing	nada
grow	creciendo	fear	temer
friends	amigos	hour	hora
laughing	reír	laden	llena
sharing	compartir	love	amor
family	familia	second	segundo
loving	amor	comfort	consolación
caring	cariño	above	cielo
kindness	bondad	living	vivir